1ST GRADE PHONICS
Unit 8
Spelling Vowel Teams

MW01593370

TABLE OF CONTENTS

IMPORTANT: Please refer to the Teacher Guide for specific scripts, procedures, and words that are represented by pictures.

Throughout this Unit, learners will scan QR codes. Be careful they scan each code individually.

LEARN

- Spelling vowel team words
- Dividing and reading vowel team words
- ABC order by first and second letters

DAILY PAGE GOALS

Day	Complete	Day	Complete	Day	Complete
1	ii–7	7	35–40	13	67–72
2	8–16	8	41–47	14	73–79
3	17–23	9	48–55	15	80–86
4	24–28	10	56–60	16	87–92
5	29–30	11	61–62	17	93–94
6	31–34	12	63–66	18	95–98

1. SPELLING LIST 10: Part 1

Learn:

- Read compound words with vowel team **igh**.
- Spell and read words from List 10.

WRITING PHONOGRAM REVIEW

Listen to and write the phonograms.
Underline any multi-letter phonograms.

WORKING WITH WORDS

In this Unit, you will learn how to spell more vowel teams. This Lesson has words with vowel team **igh**.

br**igh**t   l**igh**t

The word *light* is in many compound words

high**light**   head**lights**   fire**light**

Divide and read the words.
Remember, underline the multi-letter phonograms.
Write each word under the correct picture.

stop | **light**
word 1   word 2

flashlight

moonlight

sunlight

streetlight

1)

_____

- - - - - - - - - - - - - - -

_____

2)

_____

- - - - - - - - - - - - - - -

_____

3)

_____

- - - - - - - - - - - - - - -

_____

4)

_____

- - - - - - - - - - - - - - -

_____

Listen!

Circle the correct answers.

5)	syllables	1	2	3	4

6)	sounds	1	2	3	4

Write and read.

7) _____

Choose the correct answer.

8) Which reading rule does this word follow?

- ○ long **i** before two consonants
- ○ beginning **s**
- ○ 1ˢᵗ sound of **c**

4

Listen!

 **Circle the correct answers.**

| 9) | syllables | 1 | 2 | 3 | 4 |

| 10) | sounds | 1 | 2 | 3 | 4 |

 **Write and read.**

11) _____

 **Choose the correct answer.**

12) What is the syllable type?
   ○ VCe
   ○ open
   ○ vowel team

Listen!

Circle the correct answers.

| 13) | syllables | 1 | 2 | 3 | 4 |

| 14) | sounds | 1 | 2 | 3 | 4 |

Write and read.

15) _____

Choose the correct answer.

16) The vowel sound is _____.
- ○ long
- ○ short
- ○ r-controlled

Choose the correct answers.

17) Mark (☒) TWO words that rhyme.

　□ right　　　　　□ sight　　　　　□ high

Write the correct answers.
Complete the sentences.

right	sight	high

18) The plane flew _____ in the sky.

19) I looked out the window on my _____ side.

20) The _____ of all those clouds was great!

SCORE　　　CORRECT　　　RESCORE

Learn:

- Read words with vowel team **oo**.

- Spell and read words from List 10.

WRITING PHONOGRAM REVIEW

Listen to and write the phonograms.
Underline any multi-letter phonograms.

WORKING WITH WORDS

This Lesson has words with vowel team **oo**. Vowel team **oo** has two sounds. Most of the time, the first sound is only used before the letters **k**, **d**, or **t**. The second sound can be used in any position.

1ˢᵗ Sound of **oo**	2ⁿᵈ Sound of **oo**

b**oo**k

z**oo**

Brooklyn was looking for a good book. She looked under her foot. She looked under the hood of a car. Then, she went to the woods to look. She ran into a good pal. She asked, "Do you know how to find a good book?"

Cooper said, "That's a goofy thing to ask! The school has a big room full of them! I am on my way to the zoo. Want to go with me?"

Soon, the two pals made it to the zoo. They heard a cow say "Moo!" They watched a toothy walrus splash in a pool. When they left, they each got a cool balloon.

 **Choose the correct answers.**

1) What was Brooklyn looking for?
   ○ a good book
   ○ her pal Cooper
   ○ a cool balloon

2) Where did Cooper and Brooklyn go?

to the zoo   to school   to the pool

3) What sound did Cooper and Brooklyn hear?
   ○ Moo!
   ○ Boo!
   ○ Hoot!

Listen!

 **Circle the correct answers.**

| 4) | syllables | 1 | 2 | 3 | 4 |

| 5) | sounds | 1 | 2 | 3 | 4 |

 **Write and read.**

6) _____

 **Choose the correct answer.**

7) What is the syllable type?

    O vowel team

    O closed

    O r-controlled

Listen!

 **Circle the correct answers.**

| 8) | syllables | 1 | 2 | 3 | 4 |

| 9) | sounds | 1 | 2 | 3 | 4 |

 **Write and read.**

10) _____

 **Choose the correct answer.**

11) The vowel makes its ____ sound.
   ○ first
   ○ third
   ○ second

Listen!

Circle the correct answers.

| 12) | syllables | 1 | 2 | 3 | 4 |

| 13) | sounds | 1 | 2 | 3 | 4 |

Write and read.

14) _____

Choose the correct answer.

15) The vowel makes its ____ sound.
   ○ third
   ○ first
   ○ second

Listen!

? **Circle the correct answers.**

16) syllables   1   2   3   4

17) sounds   1   2   3   4

✏️ **Write and read.**

18) _____

? **Choose the correct answer.**

19) Which position is the vowel in?
   - ○ beginning
   - ○ middle
   - ○ ending

? Choose the correct answers.

20) Mark (☒) TWO words that make the second sound of **oo**.

☐ too ☐ moon ☐ took

✏ Write the correct answers.
Sort the words in ABC order.

too	foot	moon

21) _____

22) _____

23) _____

✏ Use the word in your own sentence.

took

24) _____

3. SPELLING LIST 10: Part 3

Learn:

- Read words with vowel team **ea**.

- Spell and read words from List 10.

WRITING PHONOGRAM REVIEW

Listen to and write the phonograms.
Underline any multi-letter phonograms.

17

WORKING WITH WORDS

This Lesson has words with vowel team **ea**. Its first sound is the long **e** sound. We use it in many one-syllable words

Read, sort, and write the words.
Meal words are about food and drinks. *Beach* words are about water and the outdoors.

| tea | sea | heat | eat |
| seal | feast | stream | beans |

1) **Meal Words**

2) **Beach Words**

Listen!

 **Circle the correct answers.**

3) | syllables | 1 2 3 4

4) | sounds | 1 2 3 4

 **Write and read.**

5) _____

 **Choose the correct answer.**

6) What is the syllable type?
   - ○ VCe
   - ○ open
   - ○ vowel team

Listen!

Circle the correct answers.

7)

syllables	1	2	3	4

8)

sounds	1	2	3	4

Write and read.

9) _____

Choose the correct answer.

10) Which reading rule does this word follow?
   ○ middle **s**
   ○ beginning **s**
   ○ 1st sound of **c**

Listen!

 **Circle the correct answers.**

| 11) | syllables | 1 | 2 | 3 | 4 |

| 12) | sounds | 1 | 2 | 3 | 4 |

 **Write and read.**

13) _____

 **Choose the correct answer.**

14) The vowel sound is ____.
- ○ long
- ○ short
- ○ r-controlled

15) Chelsea and Neal **eat** their lunches.

16) Jean saw a boat on the **sea.**

17) **Each** child has a seat.

SCORE   CORRECT   RESCORE

ACTIVITY: Writing Words

Read, trace, and write the words.

Read	Trace	Write
sight	sight	
high	high	
right	right	
took	took	
foot	foot	
moon	moon	
too	too	
eat	eat	
sea	sea	
each	each	

PHONOGRAM REVIEW

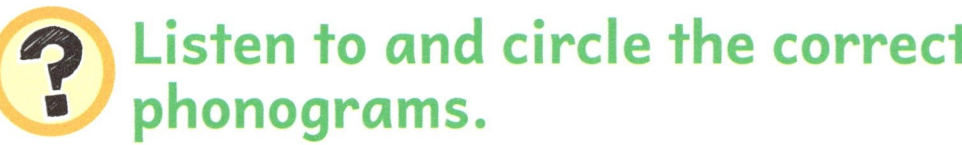

Listen to and circle the correct phonograms.

1) gn   kn   ng

2) oo   ui   o

3) ear   ar   er

4) p   l   m

5) ea   ee   e

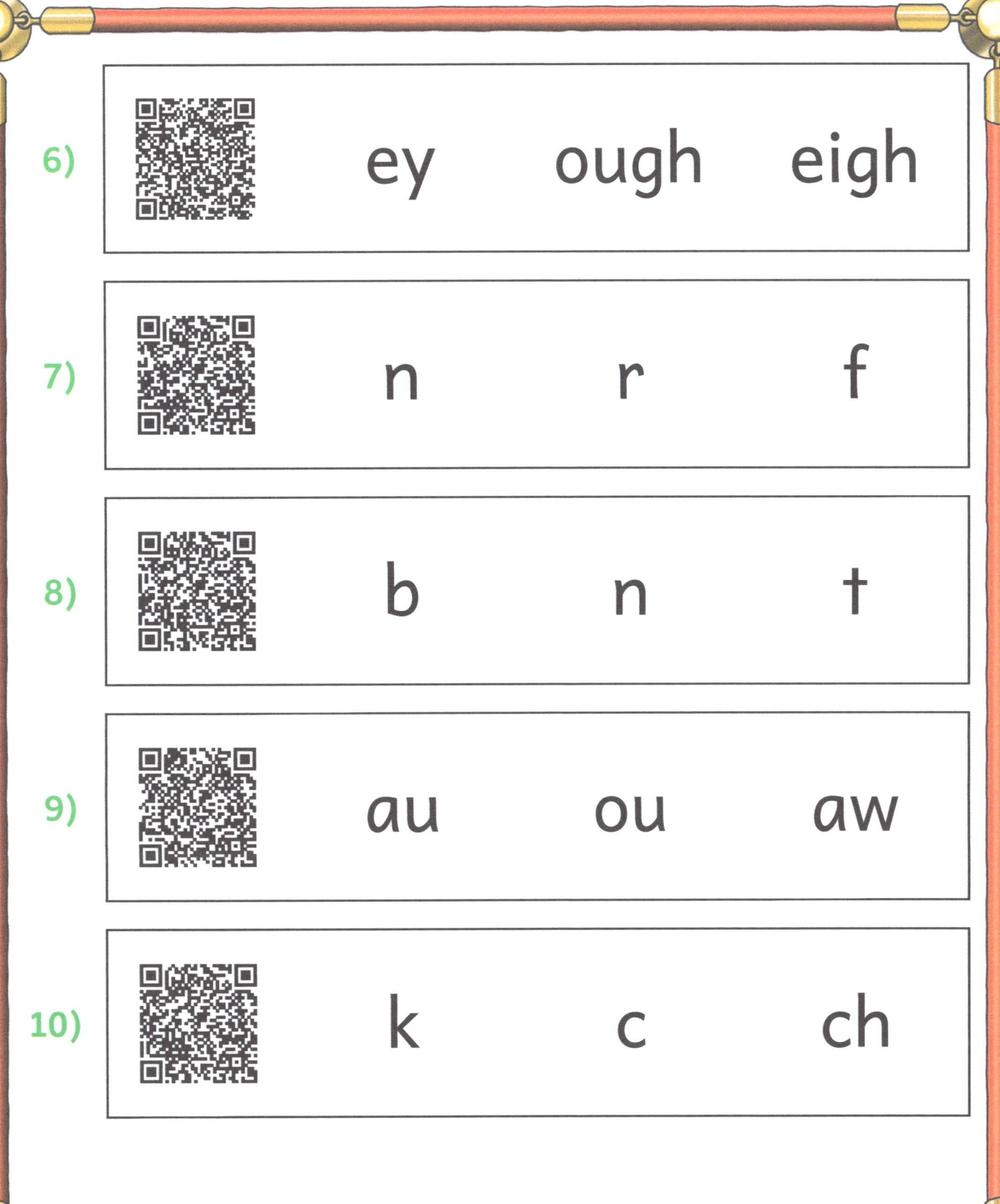

6) ey   ough   eigh

7) n   r   f

8) b   n   t

9) au   ou   aw

10) k   c   ch

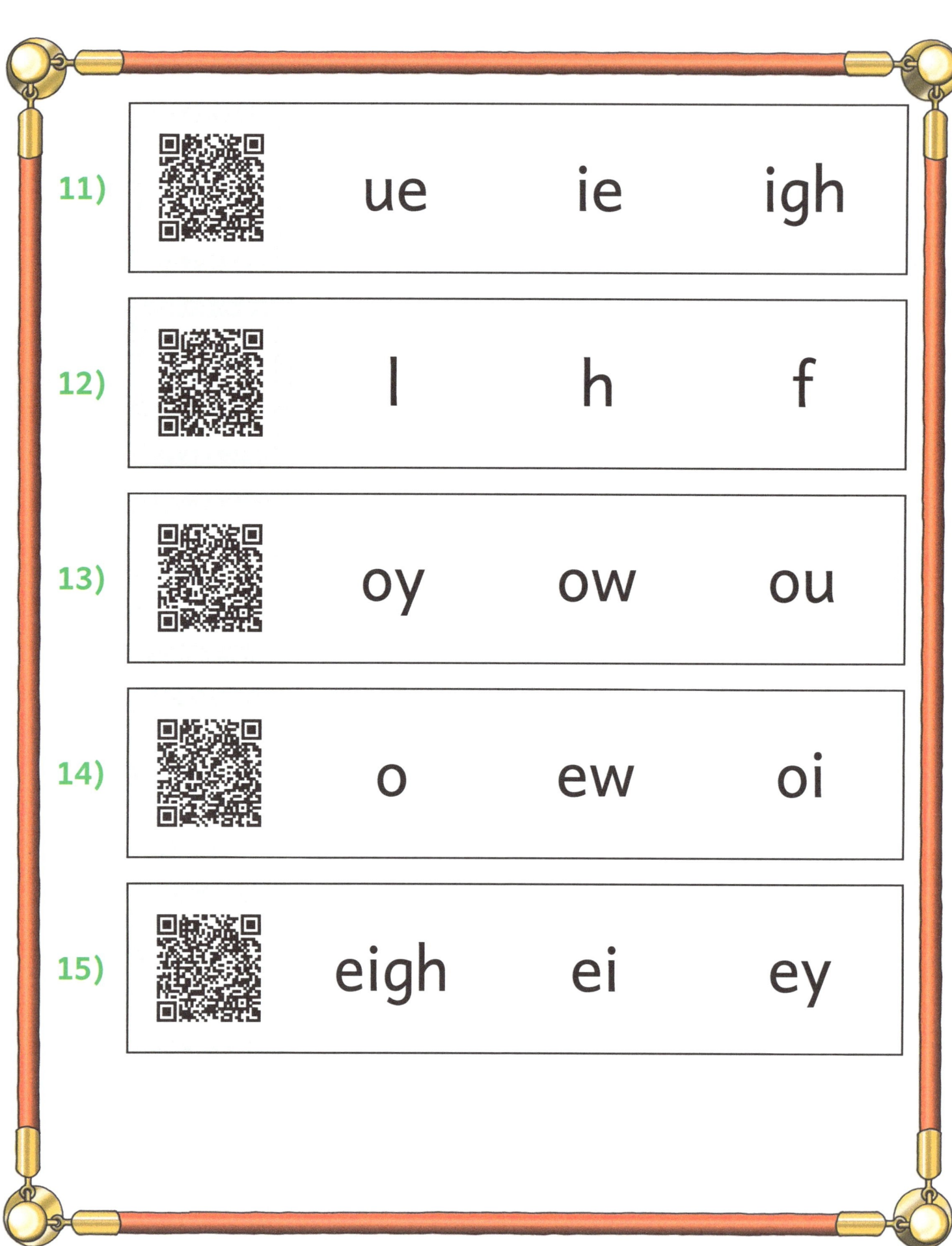

11) ue ie igh

12) l h f

13) oy ow ou

14) o ew oi

15) eigh ei ey

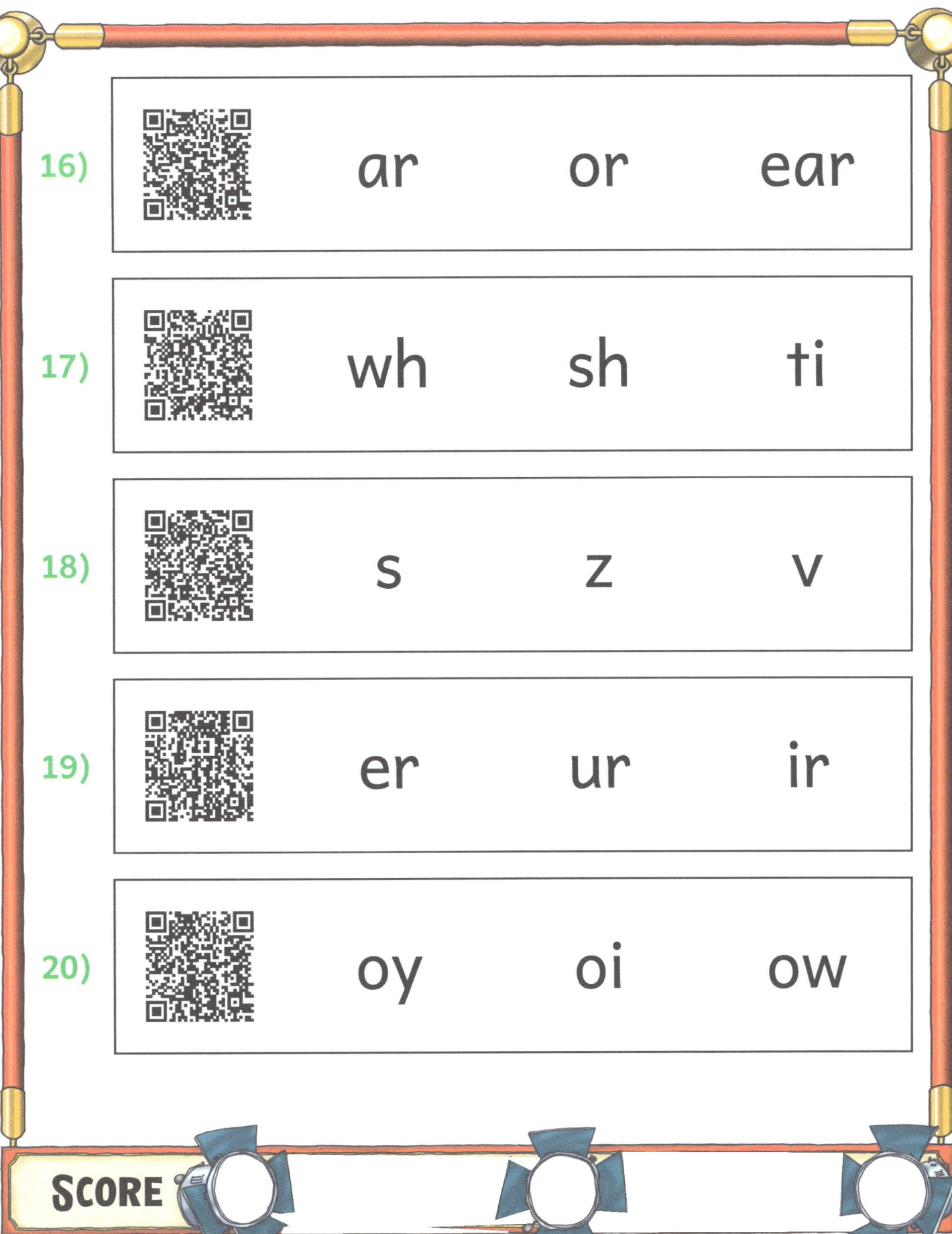

16)   ar   or   ear

17)   wh   sh   ti

18)   s   z   v

19)   er   ur   ir

20)   oy   oi   ow

SCORE

SPELLING LIST 10 REVIEW

 **Write the correct answers.**
Write the words in the boxes.

sight   took   high   eat   moon

1)

2)

3)
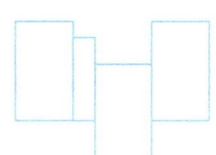

4)

5)
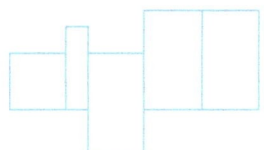

right   foot   each   sea   too

6)

7)

8)

9)

10)

This Reader has the tricky word *gone*. It ends with silent final **e**, but the letter **o** makes its short sound. *Gone* is a form of *go*.

Tricky Word
gone

 **Listen to the forms of *go* in this sentence.**

We will **go** look at stars after the sun **goes** down and all the light is **gone**.

 **Write the correct answers.**
Complete the sentences.

go	goes	gone

1) The teapot _____ on the top shelf.

2) The new book was _____ when I got to the shop.

3) Dwight wants to _____ see the play.

Reader 17
Pip and His Wild Dreams

Choose the correct answers.

4) Where did Pip sleep?
- ○ on the moon
- ○ on a plane
- ○ by the sea

5) What was made of candy?
- ○ the clouds
- ○ the moon
- ○ the stars

6) Which dream did Pip like the most?
- ○ being a rock star
- ○ jumping in mud
- ○ flying to the moon

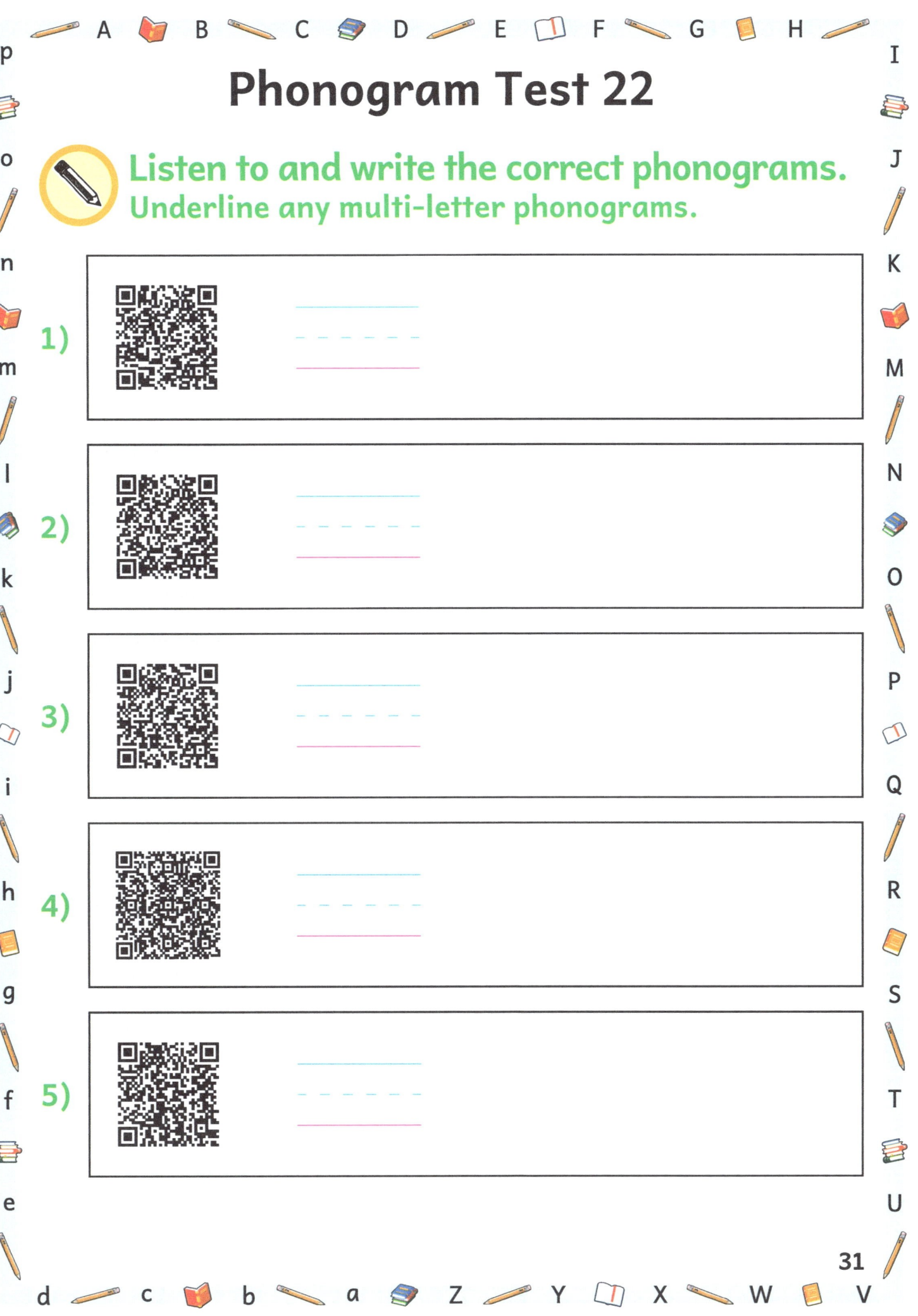

Phonogram Test 22

Listen to and write the correct phonograms.
Underline any multi-letter phonograms.

1)

2)

3)

4)

5)

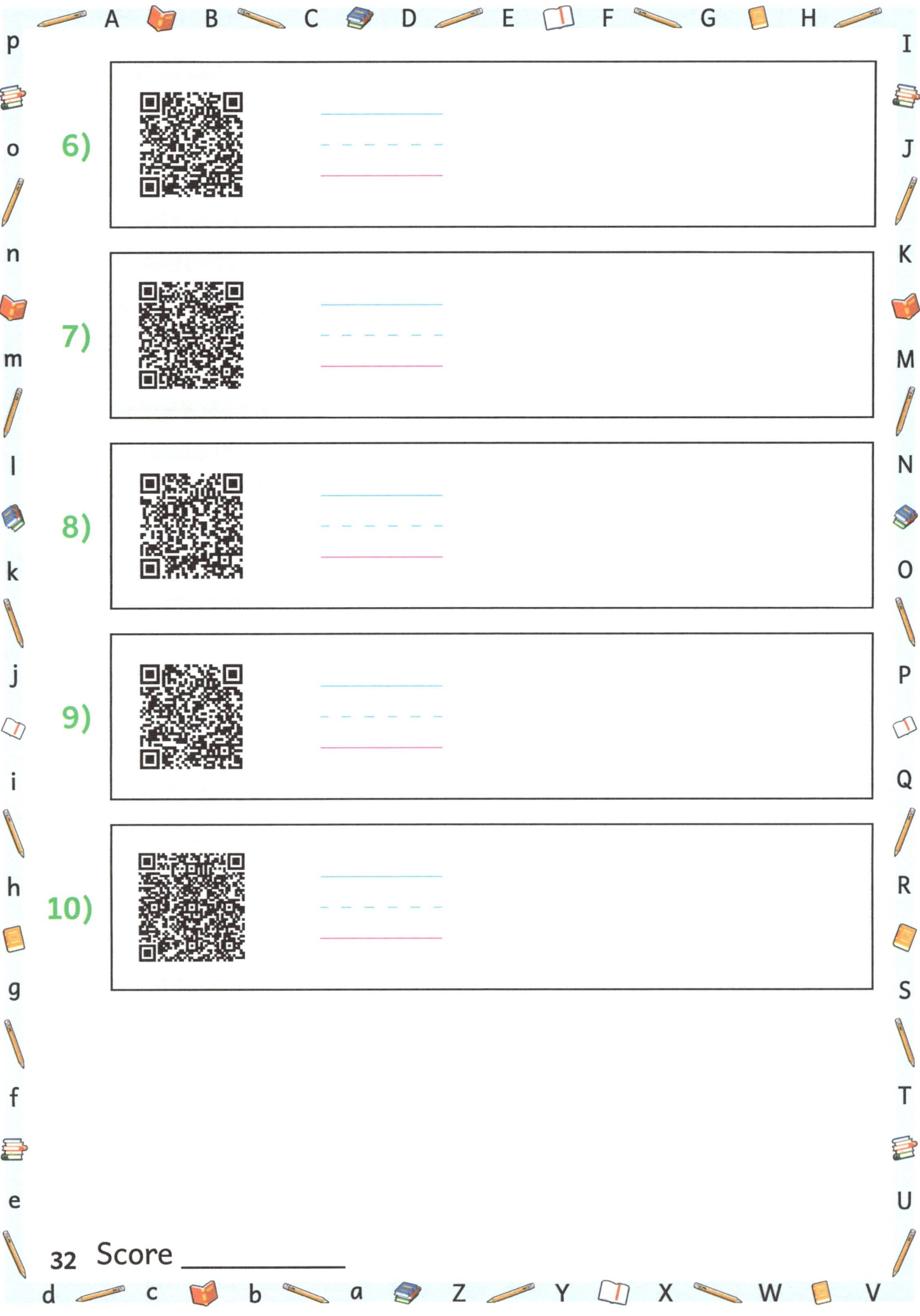

Score _____

Spelling Test List 10

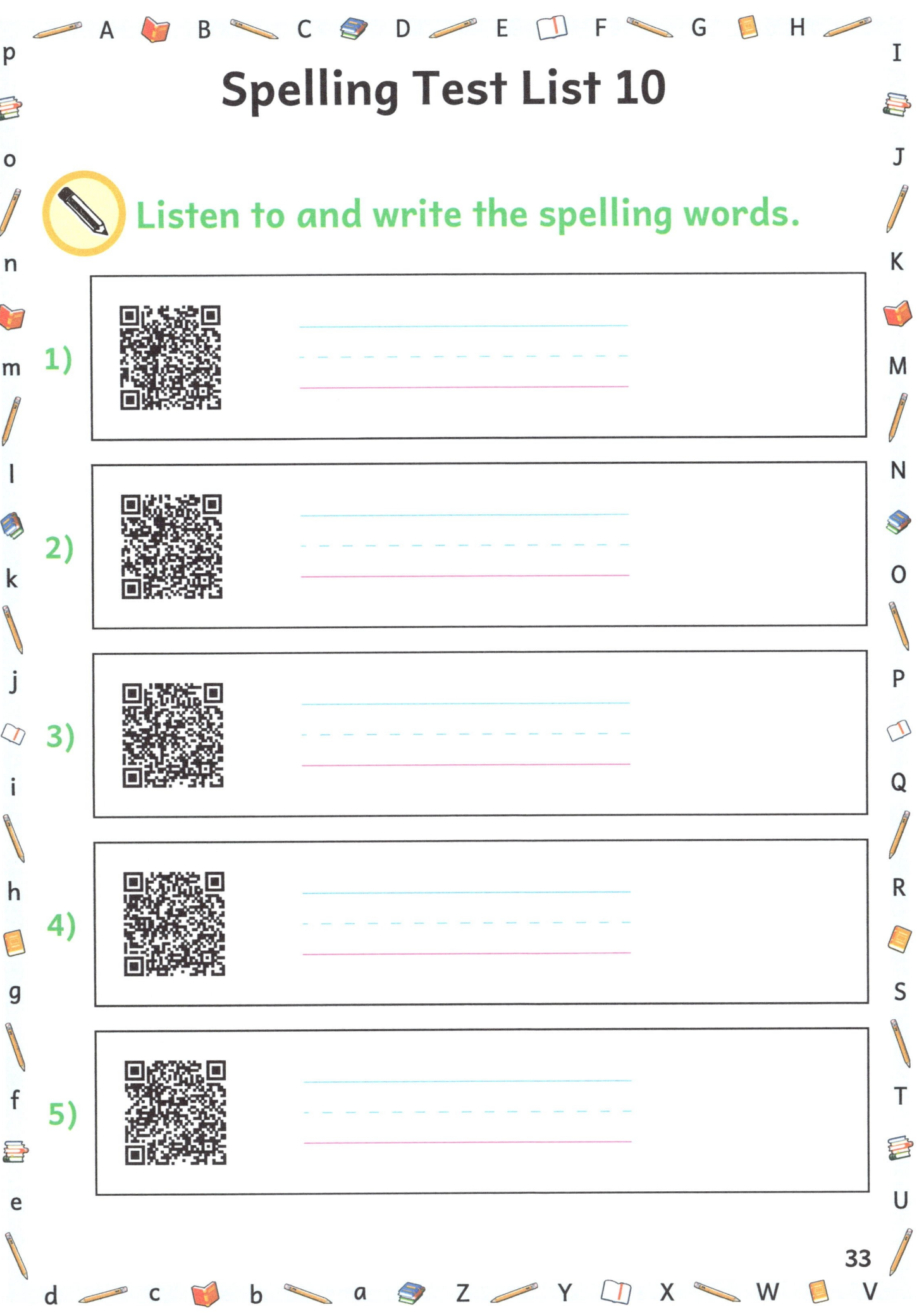

Listen to and write the spelling words.

1)

2)

3)

4)

5)

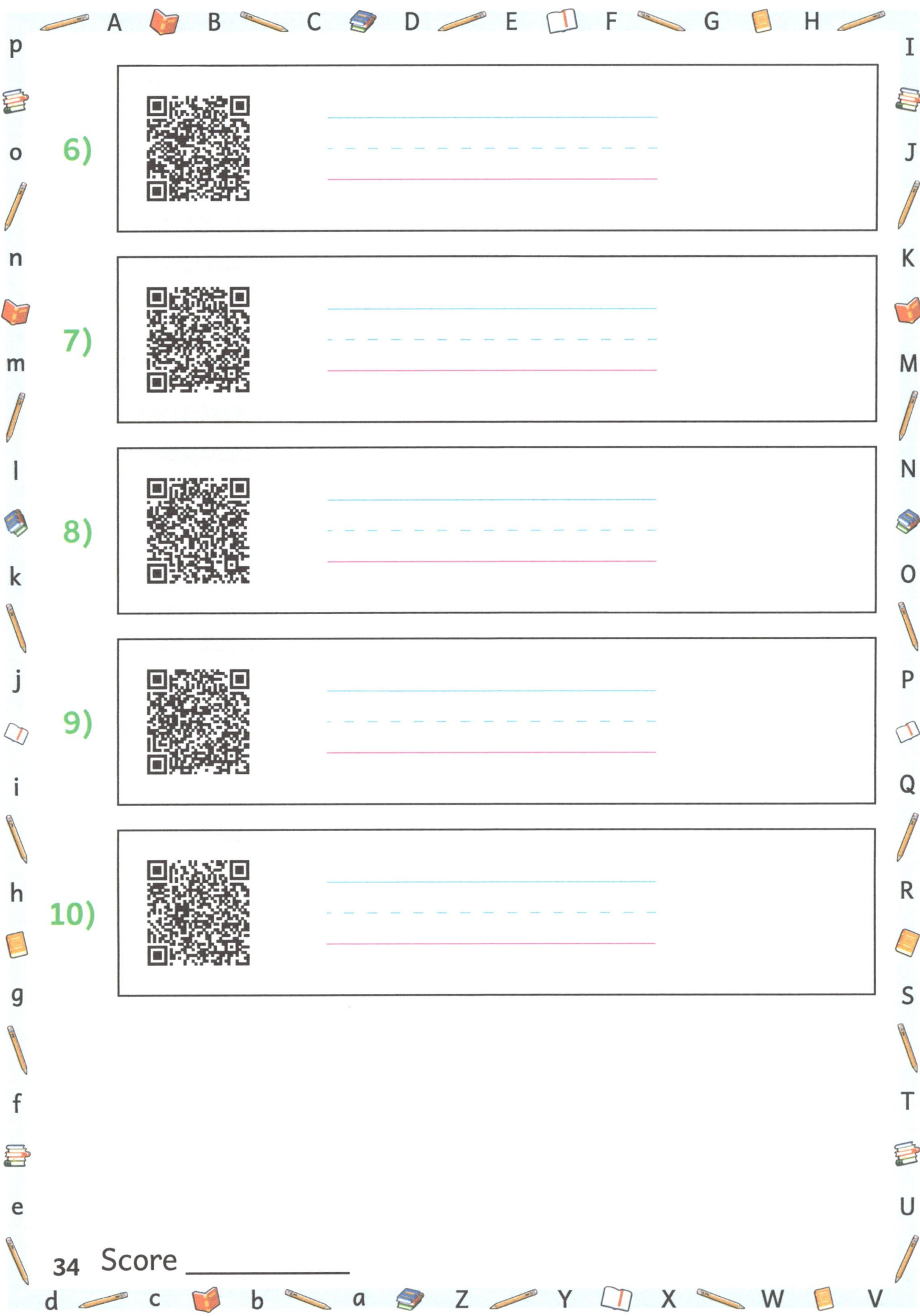

Score _____

4. SPELLING LIST 11: Part 1

Learn:

- Divide and read words with long **a** sounds.

- Spell and read words from List 11.

WRITING PHONOGRAM REVIEW

✏️ **Listen to and write the phonograms.**
Underline any multi-letter phonograms.

WORKING WITH WORDS

Spelling List 11 has words with vowel teams **ai** and **ay**. They make the long **a** sound. Vowel team **ay** is used at the end of words. Vowel team **ai** is not.

 **Write the missing letters in each word.**

1) 
spr_____

2) 
n___l

3) 
ch_____n

4) 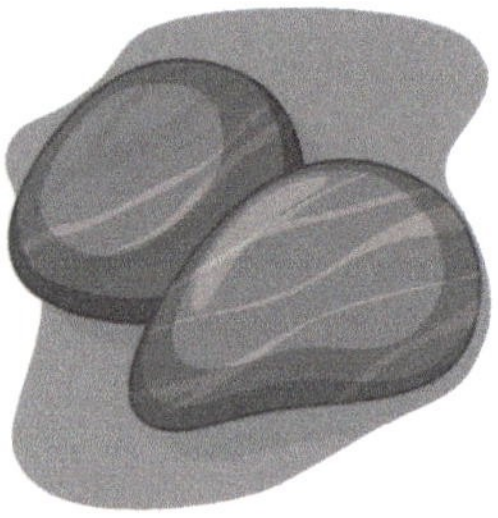
gr_____

5) 
p_____

6) 
tr_____n

7) 
pl_____

8) 
st_____rs

Listen!

 **Circle the correct answers.**

9) | syllables | 1 | 2 | 3 | 4 |

10) | sounds | 1 | 2 | 3 | 4 |

 **Write and read.**

11) _____

 **Choose the correct answer.**

12) What is the syllable type?
- ○ r-controlled
- ○ VCe
- ○ vowel team

Listen!

 **Circle the correct answers.**

13)	syllables	1	2	3	4

14)	sounds	1	2	3	4

 **Write and read.**

15) _____

 **Choose the correct answer.**

16) The vowel sound is ____.
   ○ short
   ○ long
   ○ r-controlled

Listen!

 **Circle the correct answer.**

17)

| syllables | 1 | 2 | 3 | 4 |

 **Circle the correct answers.**
Then, write each syllable.

18) syllable 1

sounds 1 2 3 4

_____

19) syllable 2

sounds 1 2 3 4

_____

 **Write and read.**

20) _____

 **Choose the correct answer.**

21) Which word has two syllables?

    ○ rain   ○ afraid   ○ mail

Circle the correct answers.
Which picture describes the sentence?

22) The news said it will **rain** today.

23) My dog is **afraid** of taking a bath.

24) Bailey likes to check the **mail** after school.

SCORE   CORRECT   RESCORE

Learn:

- Read words with suffix **ing**.

- Spell and read words from List 11.

WRITING PHONOGRAM REVIEW

Listen to and write the phonograms.
Underline any multi-letter phonograms.

WORKING WITH WORDS

Suffix **ing** means that something is happening right now.

Write the correct answers.
Read each word. Circle its suffix. Write its base word.

1) saying _____

2) fainting _____

3) braiding _____

4) paying _____

5) staying _____

6) sailing _____

7) aiming _____

8) playing _____

9) painting _____

10) spraying _____

Listen!

? Circle the correct answers.

11)

syllables	1	2	3	4

12)

sounds	1	2	3	4

✏️ Write and read.

13) _____

? Choose the correct answer.

14) What is the syllable type?
- ○ VCe
- ○ open
- ○ vowel team

Listen!

 **Circle the correct answers.**

| 15) | syllables | 1 | 2 | 3 | 4 |

| 16) | sounds | 1 | 2 | 3 | 4 |

 **Write and read.**

17) _____

 **Choose the correct answer.**

18) Which reading rule does this word follow?
   - ○ 3rd sound of **y**
   - ○ beginning **s**
   - ○ 1st sound of **c**

Listen!

Circle the correct answers.

| 19) | syllables | 1 | 2 | 3 | 4 |

| 20) | sounds | 1 | 2 | 3 | 4 |

Write and read.

21) _____

Choose the correct answer.

22) The vowel sound is ____.
- ○ short
- ○ r-controlled
- ○ long

Listen!

 **Circle the correct answer.**

23)

syllables	1	2	3	4

 **Circle the correct answers.**
Then, write each syllable.

24)

syllable 1	
sounds	1 2 3 4
	_____

25)

syllable 2	
sounds	1 2 3 4
	_____

 **Write and read.**

26) _____

? Choose the correct answer.

27) Which word has two syllables?

○ away ○ tray ○ say

✏ Write the correct answers.
Sort the words in ABC order.

tray say away

28) _____

29) _____

30) _____

✏ Use the word in your own sentence.

day

31) _____

SCORE CORRECT RESCORE

Learn:

- Read and sort words with vowel team **ie**.

- Spell and read words from List 11.

WRITING PHONOGRAM REVIEW

Listen to and write the phonograms.
Underline any multi-letter phonograms.

WORKING WITH WORDS

The words in this Lesson have vowel team **ie**. Let's review the reading rules for one-syllable words with vowel team **ie**.

1ˢᵗ Sound of **ie**	2ⁿᵈ Sound of **ie**

p**ie**   fl**ie**s

Used at the end of a base word and in suffixes **ies** and **ied**.

y**ie**ld

Used in the middle of a base word.

Write the correct answers.

Read and sort the words by the 1st and 2nd ie sound.

chief	fries	brief	tie
tried	shield	shriek	skies

1) 1st Sound of **ie**

2) 2nd Sound of **ie**

50

Listen!

? Circle the correct answers.

3) | syllables | 1 | 2 | 3 | 4 |

4) | sounds | 1 | 2 | 3 | 4 |

✏️ Write and read.

5) _____

? Choose the correct answer.

6) Which position is the vowel in?
  ○ beginning
  ○ middle
  ○ ending

Listen!

? Circle the correct answers.

| 7) | syllables | 1 | 2 | 3 | 4 |

| 8) | sounds | 1 | 2 | 3 | 4 |

✏ Write and read.

9) _____

? Choose the correct answer.

10) The vowel makes its ____ sound.

　　○ first
　　○ second
　　○ third

Listen!

 **Circle the correct answers.**

11) | syllables | 1 | 2 | 3 | 4 |

12) | sounds | 1 | 2 | 3 | 4 |

 **Write and read.**

13) _____

 **Choose the correct answer.**

14) What is the syllable type?
   ○ closed
   ○ open
   ○ vowel team

❓ Choose the correct answers.

15) Mark (☒) TWO words that rhyme.

☐ lie   ☐ die   ☐ field

✏️ Write the correct answers.
Complete the sentences.

field	lie	die

16) The farmer planted corn in the _____.

17) He works hard so the plants will not _____.

18) At the end of the day, he will _____ on the couch.

ACTIVITY: Writing Words

Read, trace, and write these words.

Read	Trace	Write
rain	rain	
mail	mail	
afraid	afraid	
tray	tray	
say	say	
day	day	
away	away	
field	field	
lie	lie	

PHONOGRAM REVIEW

 **Listen to and circle the correct phonograms.**

1)  ci   sh   si

2)  oa   o   ue

3)  h   wh   igh

4)  ck   k   ch

5)  z   c   s

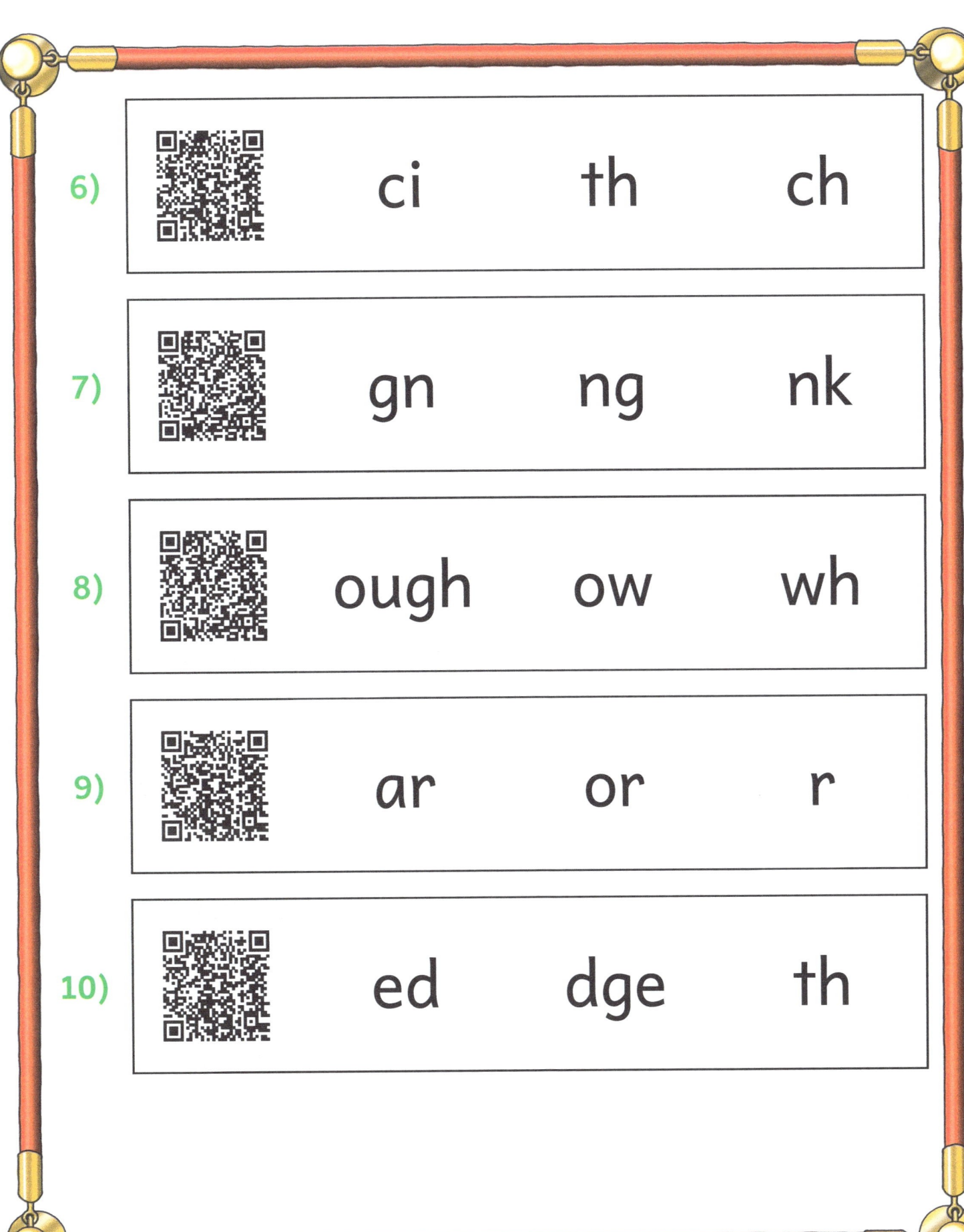

6)   ci   th   ch

7)   gn   ng   nk

8)   ough   ow   wh

9)   ar   or   r

10)   ed   dge   th

11)	tch	c	k
12)	th	ti	dge
13)	oo	oe	oa
14)	th	f	ph
15)	er	wor	or

16) ew   oo   ui

17) j   g   dge

18) d   ph   h

19) e   a   o

20) kn   nk   gn

SCORE   CORRECT   RESCORE

SPELLING LIST 11 REVIEW

We put words in ABC order by their first letter. When the first letter is the same, we have to use the second letter.

eerie	paint
essay	pie
explain	play

 **Write the correct answers.**
Sort the words in ABC order. You will need to use the second letter for some words.

rain   mail   afraid   tray   away

1) _____   3) _____   5) _____

2) _____   4) _____

day   say   field   lie   die

6) _____   8) _____   10) _____

7) _____   9) _____

This Reader has the tricky word been. The vowel team **ee** does not make its usual sound. It makes the short **i** sound. *Been* is a form of *be*.

Tricky Word
b**ee****n**

 **Listen to the forms of *be* in this sentence.**

Aiden has **been** out sick all week, so **being** back at school will **be** hard.

 **Write the correct answers.**
Complete the sentences.

be	being	been

1) Katie has _____ learning how to tie a knot.

2) Charlie wants to _____ a writer when he grows up.

3) Hayden is _____ silly today.

61

Reader 18
**Quack and Meg
Run the Mail**

? **Circle the correct answers.**

4) What was Quack afraid of?

○ spiders

○ being up high

○ the dark

5) What does Meg tell Quack to use?

○ bug spray

○ a light

○ a walking stick

6) Why does Meg bring two lights?

○ Quack was worried a light might die.

○ One light was for Quack and one was for Meg.

○ She wanted the light to be twice as bright.

Phonogram Test 23

Listen to and write the correct phonograms.
Underline any multi-letter phonograms.

1)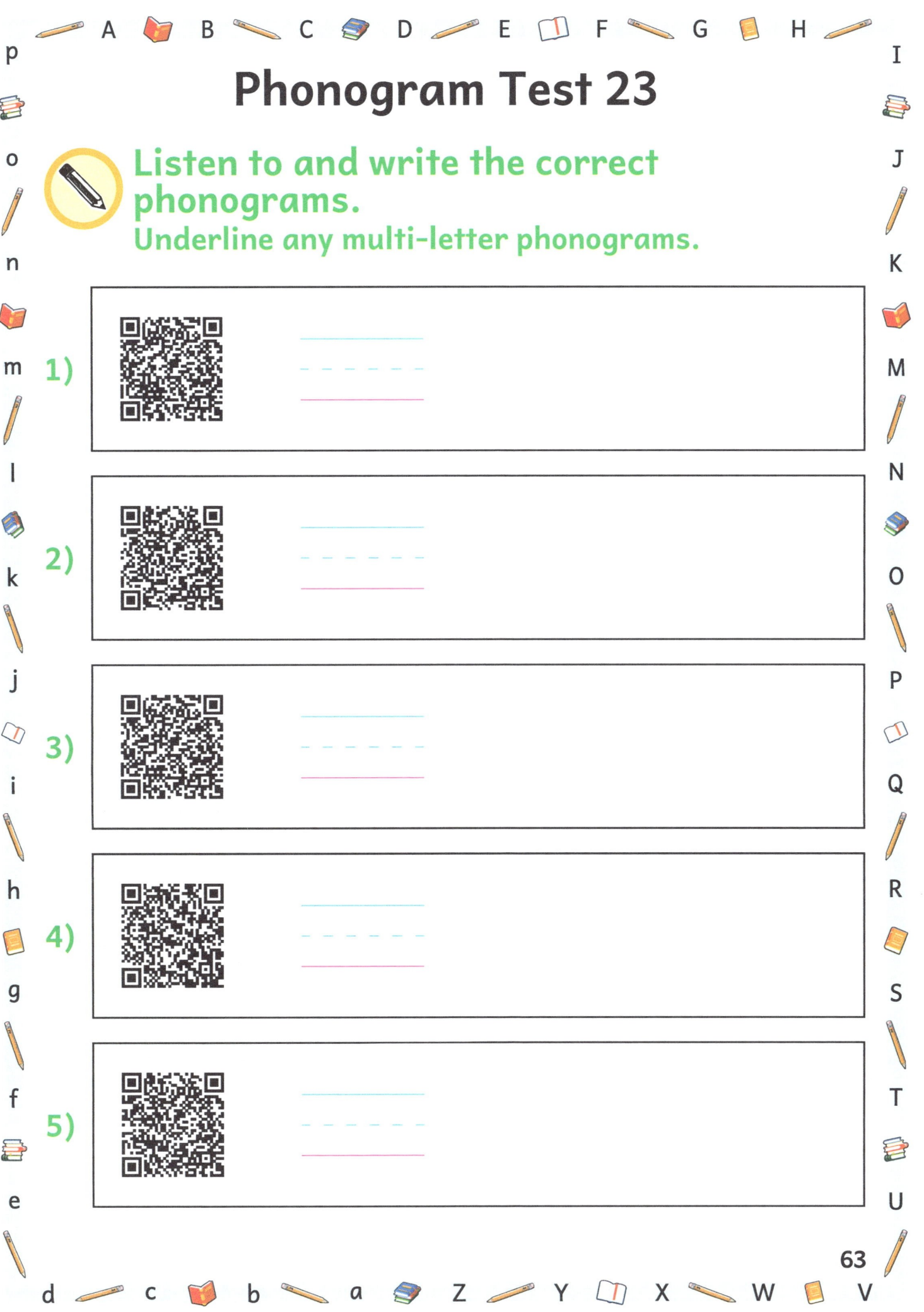

2)

3)

4)

5)

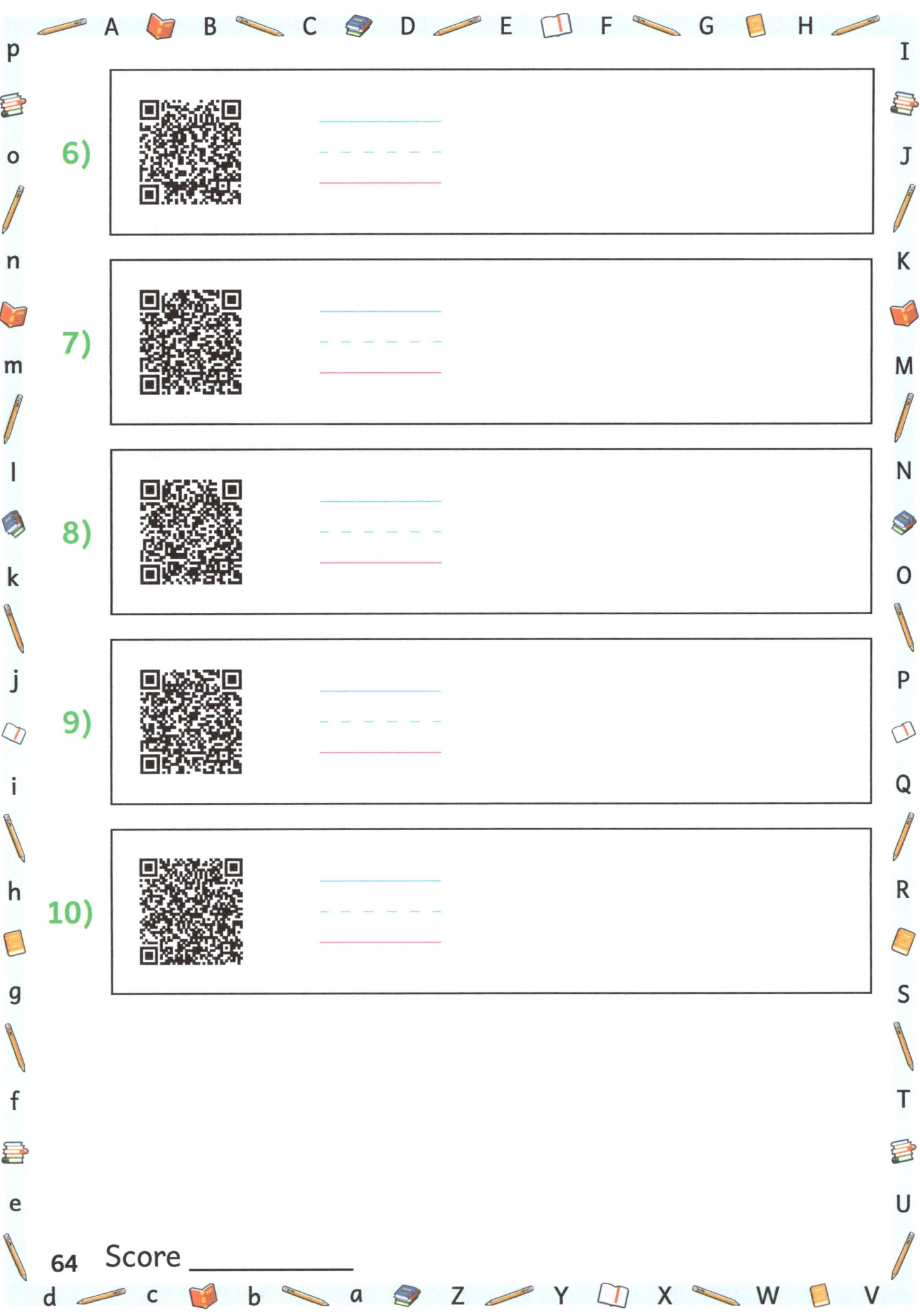

Score _____

Spelling Test List 11

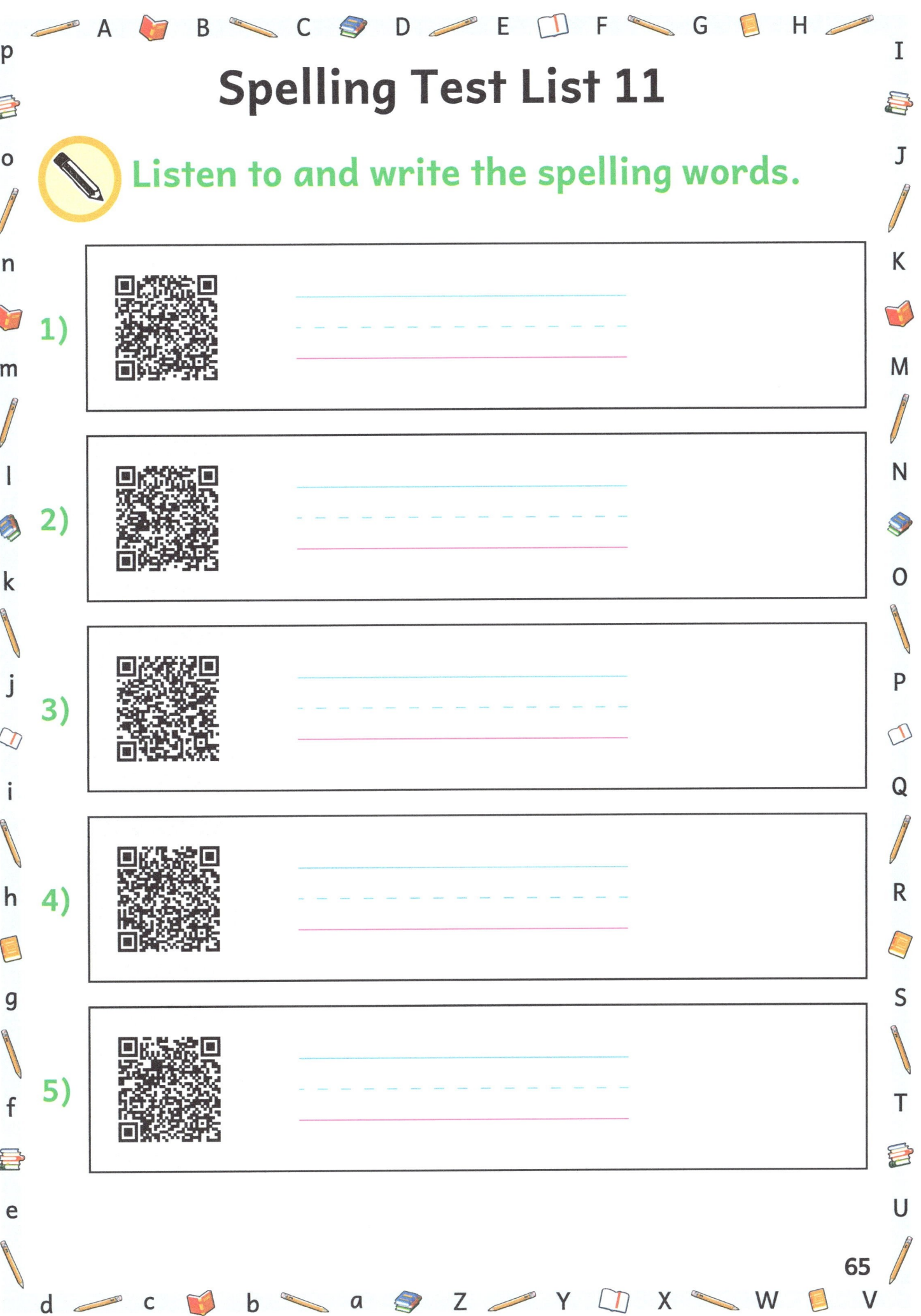

Listen to and write the spelling words.

1)

2)

3)

4)

5)

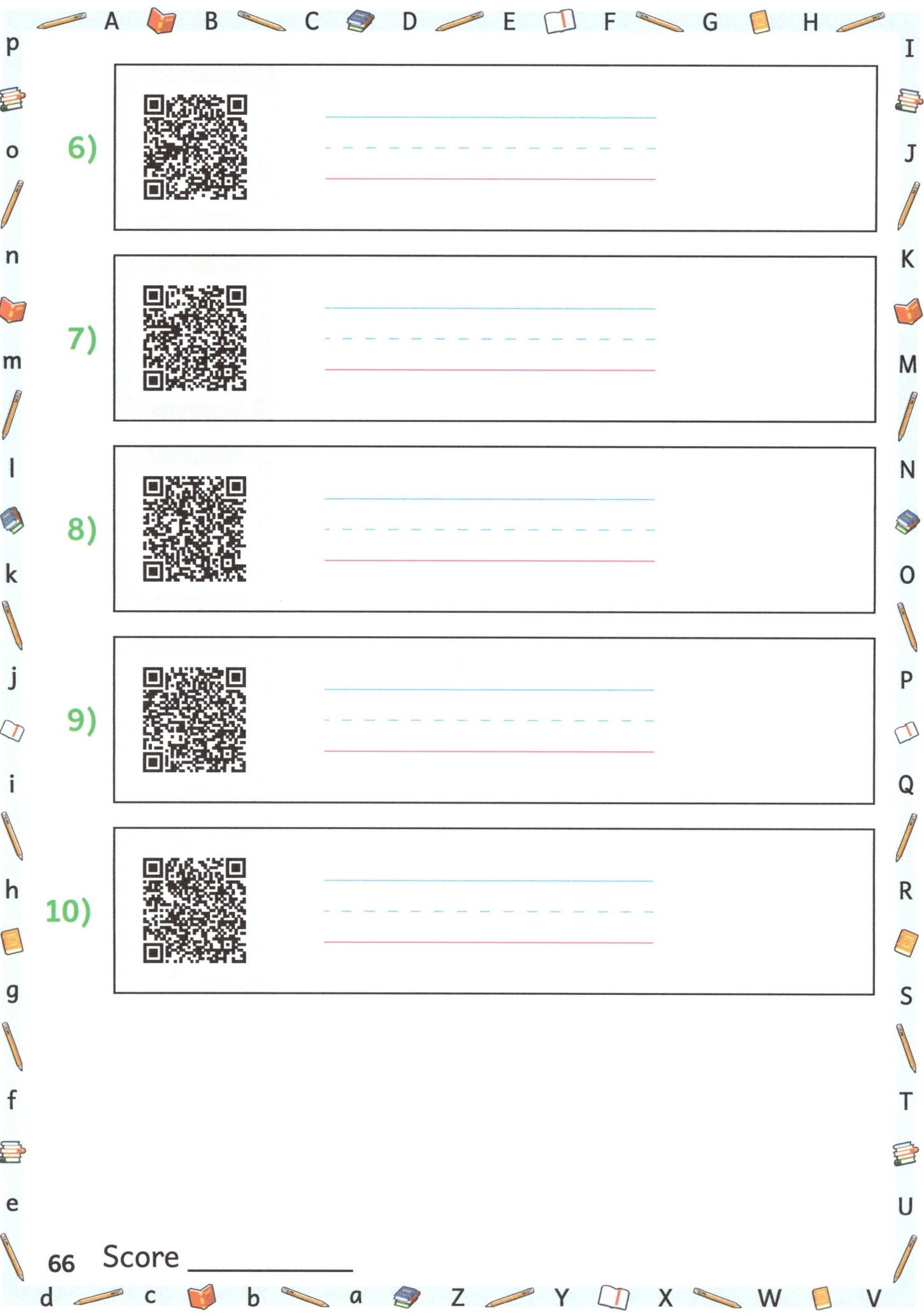

6)

7)

8)

9)

10)

Score _____

Learn:

- Read words with vowel team **ee**.

- Spell and read words from List 12.

WRITING PHONOGRAM REVIEW

Listen to and write the phonograms.
Underline any multi-letter phonograms.

WORKING WITH WORDS

This Lesson has words with vowel team **ee**. It makes the long **e** sound.

 **Circle the correct answers.**
Which sentence matches the picture?

1)

    I see green seaweed.

    I see three pinwheels.

2)

    I sleep on reindeer sheets.

    I clean the steel freezer.

3)

    I agree with a queen bee.

    I hear a tweet in the tree.

4)

    I cheer with three sheep.

    I get sneezy when I sweep.

5)

    I steer a sleek jeep.

    I peel a sweet treat.

Listen!

 **Circle the correct answers.**

6) | syllables | 1 | 2 | 3 | 4 |

7) | sounds | 1 | 2 | 3 | 4 |

 **Write and read.**

8) _____

 **Choose the correct answer.**

9) What is the syllable type?
- ○ closed
- ○ r-controlled
- ○ vowel team

Listen!

Circle the correct answer.

10) | syllables | 1 | 2 | 3 | 4 |

Circle the correct answers.
Then, write each syllable.

11) | syllable 1
sounds 1 2 3 4

_____

12) | syllable 2
sounds 1 2 3 4

_____

Write and read.

13) _____

Listen!

 **Circle the correct answers.**

| 14) | syllables | 1 | 2 | 3 | 4 |

| 15) | sounds | 1 | 2 | 3 | 4 |

 **Write and read.**

16) _____

 **Choose the correct answer.**

17) Which reading rule does this word follow?

○ beginning **s**

○ 4ᵗʰ sound of **y**

○ 1ˢᵗ sound of **c**

Write the correct answers.
Draw a line between the syllables.

18) freedom

Write the correct answers.
Complete the sentences.

freedom	sweep	keep

19) My dog enjoys the _____ to run at the dog park.

20) I tried to _____ him clean, but he got dirty.

21) My mom gave me a broom to _____ up the mess.

SCORE   CORRECT   RESCORE

Learn:

- Read words with vowel team **ou**.

- Spell and read words from List 12.

WRITING PHONOGRAM REVIEW

Listen to and write the phonograms.
Underline any multi-letter phonograms.

WORKING WITH WORDS

This Lesson has words with vowel team **ou**. It makes its first sound most of the time.

 **Write the correct answers.**
Each picture has two words that can go with it.

mouth	sound	pout	sprout
loud	hound	ground	snout

1) _____ _____

2) _____ _____

3) _____ _____

4) _____ _____

Listen!

 **Circle the correct answers.**

5) | syllables | 1 | 2 | 3 | 4 |

6) | sounds | 1 | 2 | 3 | 4 |

 **Write and read.**

7) _____

 **Choose the correct answer.**

8) What is the syllable type?
   ○ vowel team
   ○ r-controlled
   ○ VCe

Listen!

 **Circle the correct answers.**

9)	syllables	1	2	3	4

10)	sounds	1	2	3	4

 **Write and read.**

11) _____

 **Choose the correct answer.**

12) Which reading rule does this word follow?
- ○ 2nd sound of **oo**
- ○ middle **s**
- ○ 1st sound of **c**

Listen!

 **Circle the correct answers.**

| 13) | syllables | 1 | 2 | 3 | 4 |

| 14) | sounds | 1 | 2 | 3 | 4 |

 **Write and read.**

15) _____

 **Choose the correct answer.**

16) Which position is the vowel in?
   ○ beginning
   ○ middle
   ○ ending

Listen!

 **Circle the correct answers.**

17)

| syllables | 1 | 2 | 3 | 4 |

18)

| sounds | 1 | 2 | 3 | 4 |

 **Write and read.**

19) _____

 **Choose the correct answer.**

20) The vowel makes its ____ sound.
- ○ first
- ○ third
- ○ second

 **Choose the correct answer.**

21) Which word has a consonant digraph?

○ mouth   ○ our   ○ found

 **Write the correct answers.**
Sort the words in ABC order.

count	our	mouth

22) _____

23) _____

24) _____

 **Use the word in your own sentence.**

found

25) _____

SCORE   CORRECT   RESCORE

79

9. SPELLING LIST 12: Part 3

Learn:

- Make compound words with vowel team **oa**.

- Spell and read words from List 12.

WRITING PHONOGRAM REVIEW

 **Listen to and write the phonograms.**
Underline any multi-letter phonograms.

WORKING WITH WORDS

This Lesson has words with vowel team **oa**. It makes the long **o** sound. We use it in many one-syllable base words.

Write the correct answers.
Make compound words using the base words.

boat   coat   oat   load

1) _____meal

2) sail_____

3) rain_____

4) truck_____

 **Circle the correct answers.**

5) | syllables | 1 | 2 | 3 | 4 |

6) | sounds | 1 | 2 | 3 | 4 |

 **Write and read.**

7) _____

 **Choose the correct answer.**

8) What is the syllable type?
   - ○ vowel team
   - ○ VCe
   - ○ open

Listen!

Circle the correct answers.

9) | syllables | 1 | 2 | 3 | 4 |

10) | sounds | 1 | 2 | 3 | 4 |

Write and read.

11) _____

Choose the correct answer.

12) Which reading rule does this word follow?
   ○ middle **s**
   ○ 1st sound of **c**
   ○ long **u** says **oo**

Listen!

Circle the correct answers.

13) | syllables | 1 | 2 | 3 | 4 |

14) | sounds | 1 | 2 | 3 | 4 |

 **Write and read.**

15) _____

 **Choose the correct answer.**

16) The vowel sound is ____.
- ○ long
- ○ short
- ○ r-controlled

 **Choose the correct answers.**

17) Mark (☒) TWO words that rhyme.

☐ road   ☐ toad   ☐ coat

Circle the correct answers.
Which picture describes the sentence?

18) The band marched down the **road**.

19) I know how to zip my **coat**.

20) The **toad** eats the bugs in the garden.

SCORE   CORRECT   RESCORE

ACTIVITY: Writing Words

Read, trace, and write the words.

Read	Trace	Write
keep	keep	
freedom	freedom	
sweep	sweep	
found	found	
count	count	
mouth	mouth	
our	our	
road	road	
coat	coat	

PHONOGRAM REVIEW

?
Listen to and circle the correct phonograms.

1)  r   er   ir

2)  ai   ay   oi

3)  o   oo   ough

4)  ti   ci   th

5)  x   z   si

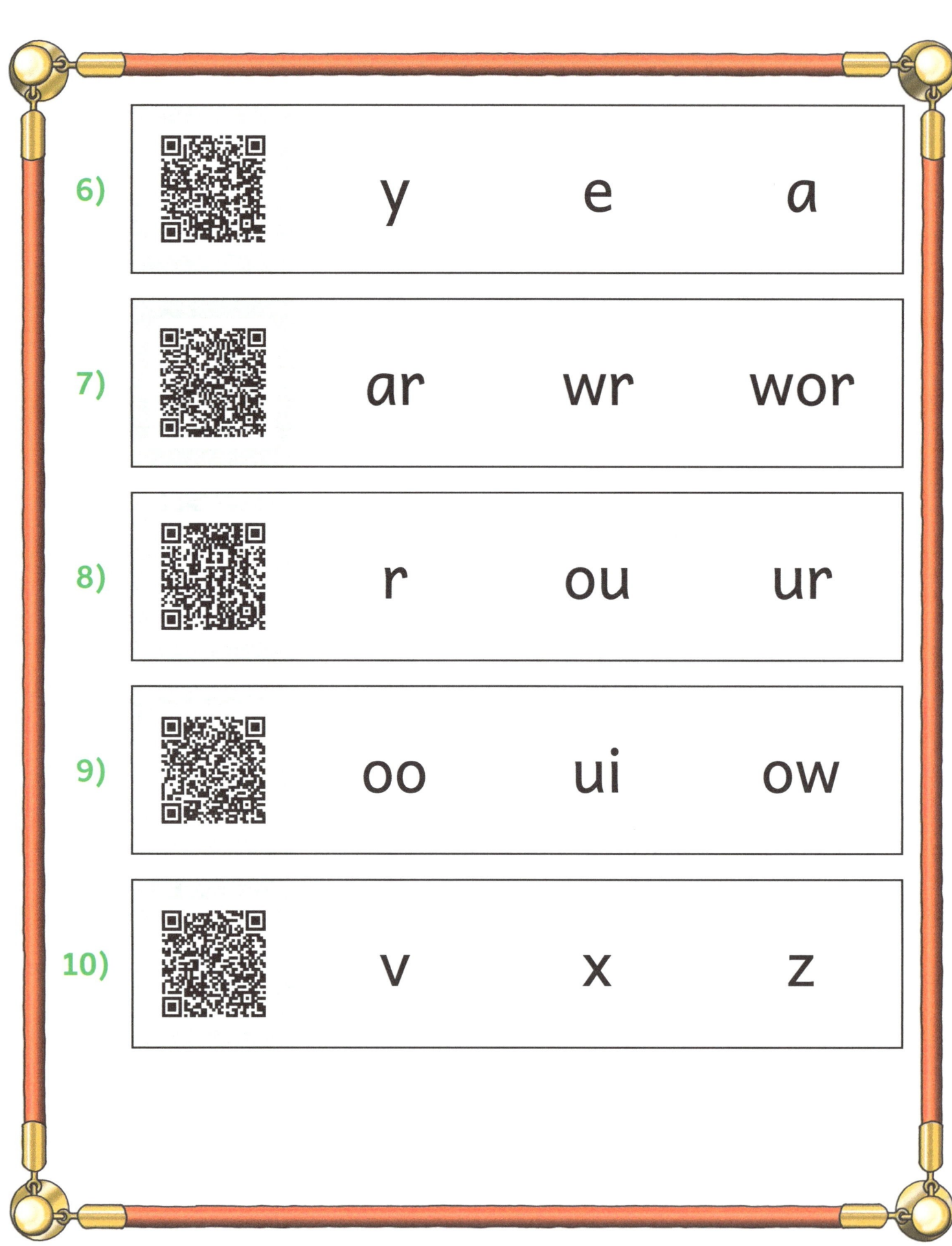

6) y   e   a

7) ar   wr   wor

8) r   ou   ur

9) oo   ui   ow

10) v   x   z

11) j   dge   y

12) or   n   r

13) o   u   i

14) tch   c   e

15) i   a   u

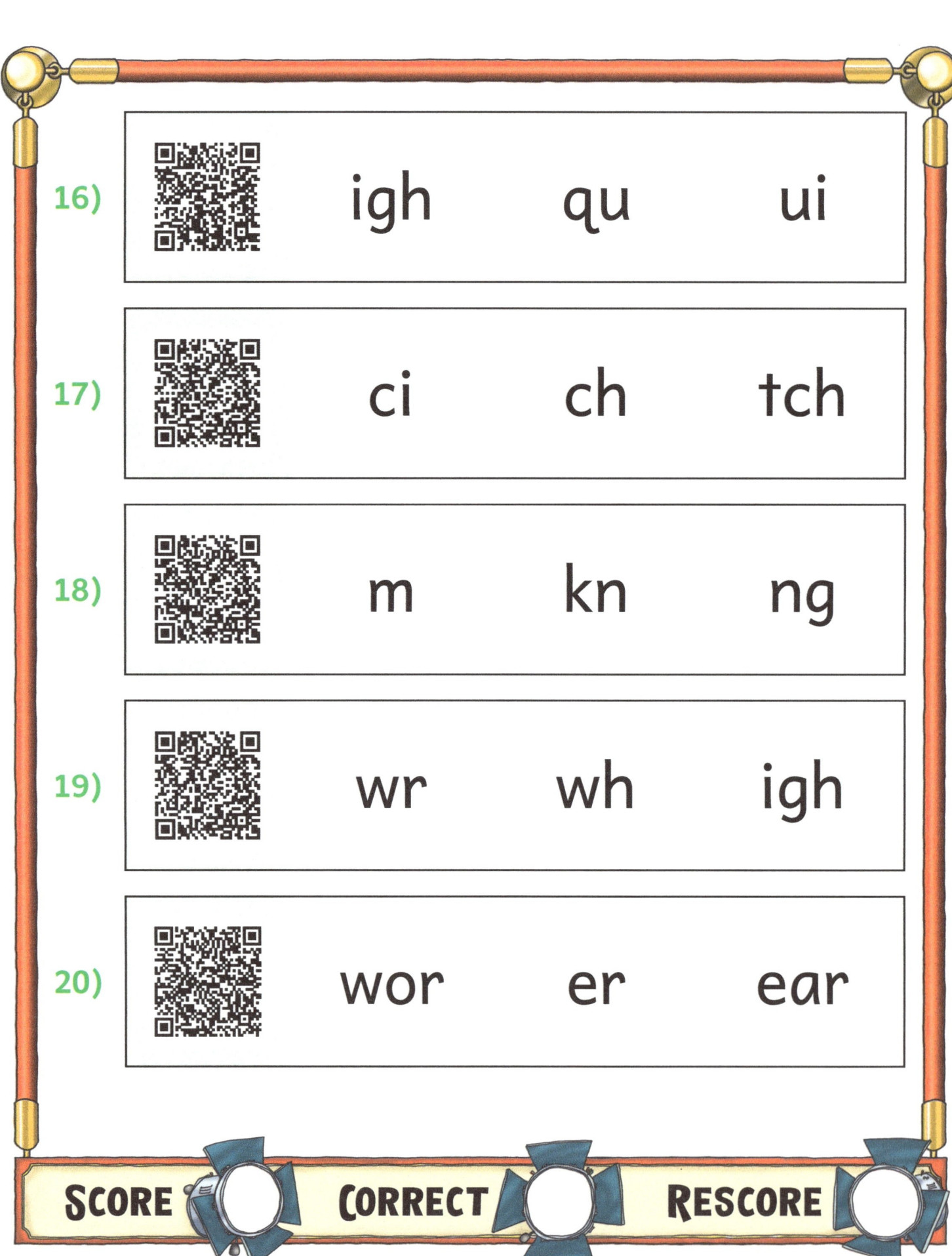

16) igh   qu   ui

17) ci   ch   tch

18) m   kn   ng

19) wr   wh   igh

20) wor   er   ear

SCORE   CORRECT   RESCORE

SPELLING LIST 12 REVIEW

 **Listen to and circle the correct words.**

1)  coat   count   found

2)  road   coat   our

3)  keep   road   coat

4)  freedom   our   found

5)  keep   sweep   coat

6) toad   found   road

7) keep   sweep   freedom

8) freedom   found   sweep

9) found   count   mouth

10) road   our   count

READER 19: "Hidden Goodies"

This Reader has the tricky word *have*. It ends with silent final **e**, but the letter **a** makes its short sound. *Have* is a form of *has*.

)))) **Listen to the forms of *has* in this sentence.**

Joan **has** a new cat, but I **have** not **had** time to go see it.

 **Write the correct answers.**
Complete the sentences.

has	have	had

1) When I was a baby, I _____ no teeth!

2) All trees _____ roots and a trunk.

1) A bee _____ four wings.

Reader 19

Hidden Goodies

Choose the correct answers.

4) What did Pip want to do with the things he found?
- ○ keep them for himself
- ○ take them to the lost and found
- ○ put them in the trash

5) Who did the three goodies belong to?
- ○ Ottie
- ○ Bix
- ○ Kit

6) What did Pip get to keep in the end?
- ○ the toad
- ○ the coat
- ○ the boat

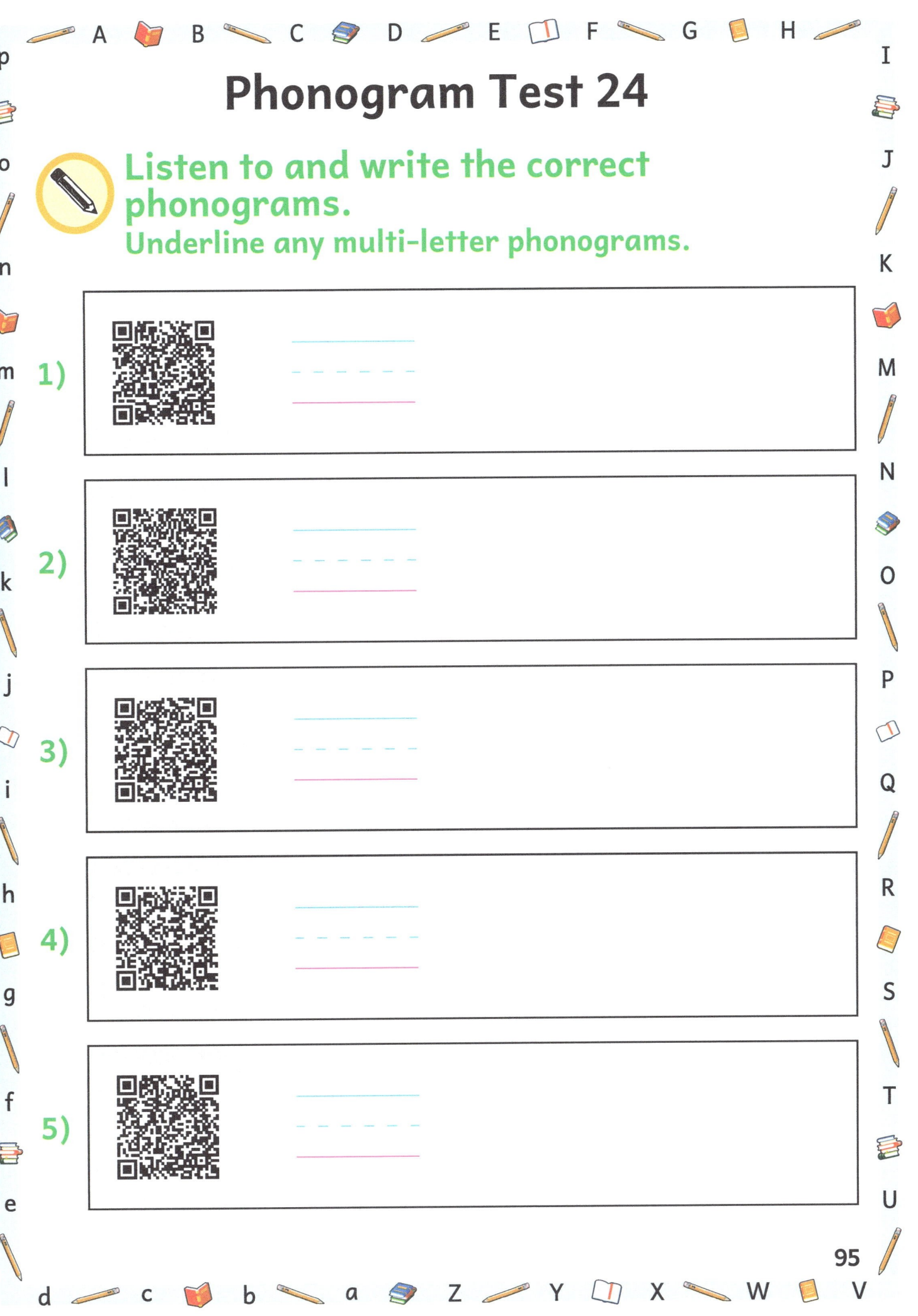

Phonogram Test 24

Listen to and write the correct phonograms.
Underline any multi-letter phonograms.

1)

2)

3)

4)

5)

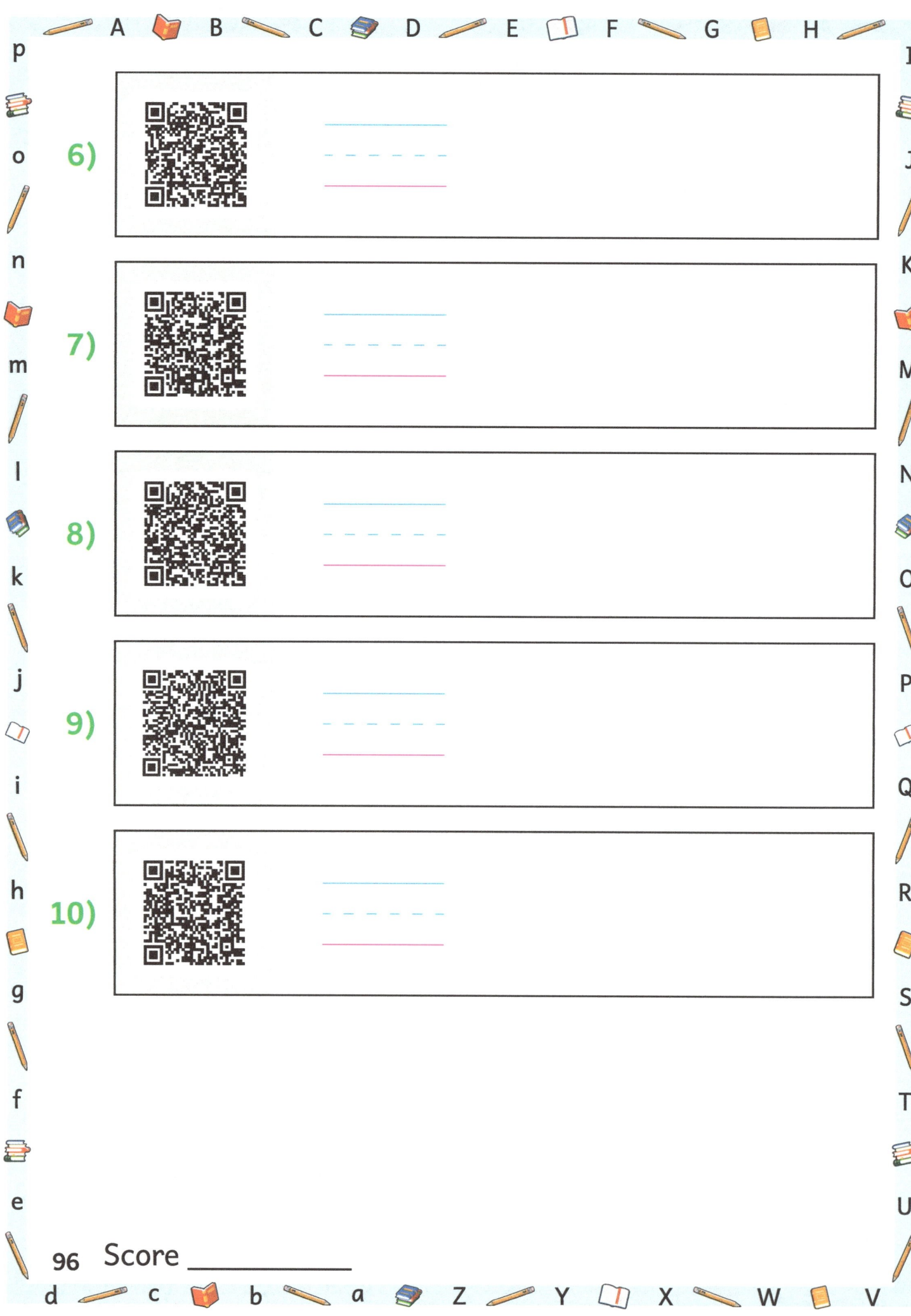

Score _____

Spelling Test List 12

Listen to and write the spelling words.

1)

2)

3)

4)

5)

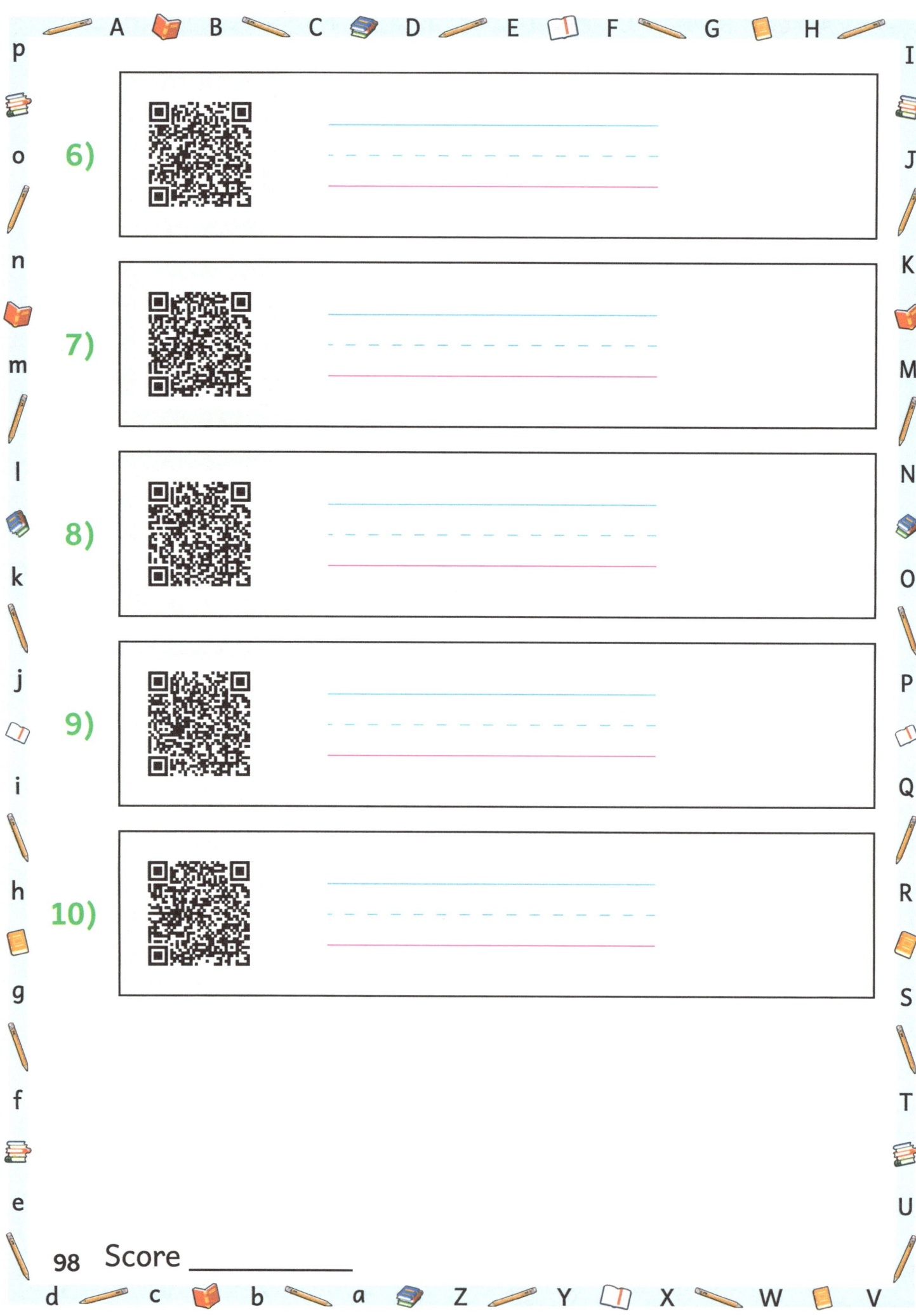

Score _____